WELCOME TO
WONDER MAMA'S ABC OF AUSTRALIA!

Join The Fabulous Wonder Mama on this visual exploration
of her homeland, Australia!

Learn about some of the unique wildlife, plantlife, landmarks,
icons, slang, and much more, that make up this country
adored by so many – within its borders and around the world!

This book is illustrated by Renny Roccon (Wonder Mama's
secret identity!) who has also published a handful of other
books including two Wonder Mama adventure stories,
and "It's OK to be ME!"

Enjoy!

THE FABULOUS
WONDER MAMA'S
ABC
OF AUSTRALIA!

Written and Illustrated by Renny Roccon
Wonder Mama Photos by Mick Tait

A

Wonder Mama lives in a country called

AUSTRALIA!

AUSTRALIA is a large island with unique **ANIMALS**, landscapes and people!

AUSTRALIAN people call themselves **"AUSSIES!"**

B

Aussies love having

BARBEQUES!

(which they call

'BARBIES')

BREKKY

is Aussie slang
for Breakfast!

C

Never smile at a **CROCODILE!**

CROCODILES are found in different parts of Australia, mainly in the north of the country! They can grow up to 4 metres long!

COCKATOOS are unique parrots! They're known for the bright yellow feathers on their head and loud screeching! There are also rare black **COCKATOOS!**

D

DIDGERIDOO

is a traditional musical wind instrument created by the Indigenous people of Australia 1000's of years ago! It is used for special ceremonies sacred to their people.

DINGOES

are wild dogs found in many parts of Australia!

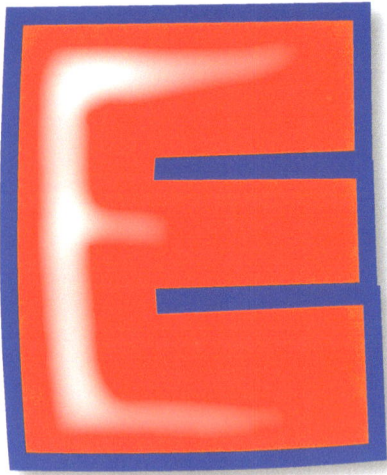

E

EMUS

are very big birds with lovely soft feathers!
They can't fly, but they can run very fast!

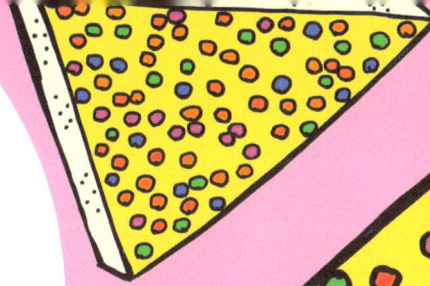

F

Aussie kids like to eat

FAIRY BREAD

at parties!

FAIRY BREAD is white bread covered with butter, sprinkled with 'Hundreds and Thousands' (colourful sprinkles) and cut into triangles! Don't forget to cut off the crusts!

G'DAY

G'DAY is what we say when we greet people! G'DAY comes from GOOD DAY!

G'DAY!

G'DAY!

G'DAY!

This is a GOANNA

H

The **HARBOUR BRIDGE** is a very big bridge in the city of Sydney! It's nickname is "The Coathanger"

ICED VO-VO

are delicious biscuits with strawberry fondant and raspberry jam topped with coconut! They're enjoyed with a 'cuppa' tea or coffee!

J

In Australia, we call sweaters or pullovers, JUMPERS!

K

KOOKABURRAS
Love to Laugh!

KOALAS
Love to Eat Gum Leaves!

KANGAROOS
Love to Jump!

They are iconic Australian animals!

L

LAMINGTON cakes are an Aussie favourite!

(Lamington cakes are sponge cake coated in chocolate, shredded coconut, with a layer of jam inside!)

In Australia sweets are called LOLLIES

M

Australia is a **MULTICULTURAL** nation.

That means people from many different cultures and countries from around the world live here together!

N

NED KELLY

was an infamous outlaw bushranger who lived hundreds of years ago. He wore metal armour to protect himself.

O

Australia is an island surrounded by **OCEAN**

...and has some of the most beautiful beaches in the world!

P

PAVLOVA
is a delicious Australian dessert made with cream, meringue and mixed berries!

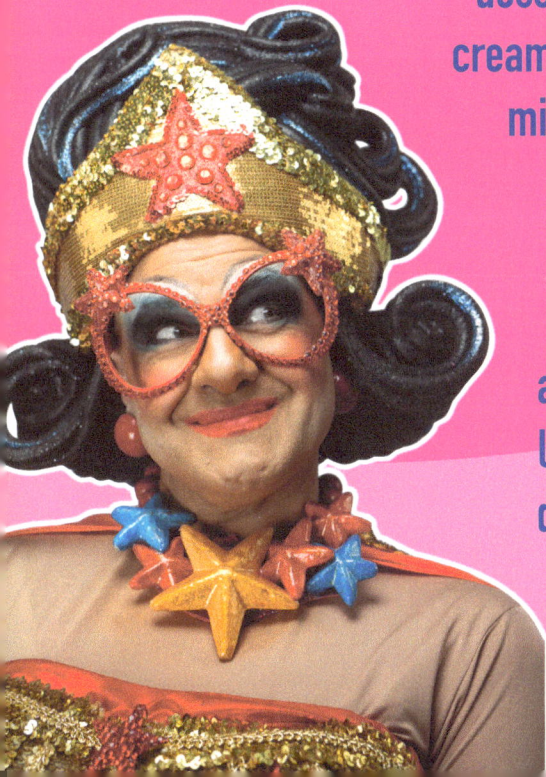

PLATYPUS
are unique water and land creatures with a duck bill and webbed feet! They are very good swimmers!

Q

QUOKKAS
are cute little furry creatures who love
to smile and are very friendly!

R

Australia's landscape includes **RAINFORESTS** and **REEFS**

RAINFORESTS are beautiful lush tropical forests with exotic plants and wildlife!

REEFS are teeming with sea life and colourful coral and sea plants!

S

SPIDERS AND SNAKES are scary critters!

Some are harmless while others can be very dangerous and poisonous!

T

THONGS
are footwear that Aussies love to wear
to the beach and anywhere else!
In other countries they call
them sandals or flip flops!

ULURU is a large rock formation in central Australia. It's a very sacred place for the Aboriginal people.

V

VEGEMITE

is a snacktime favourite in Australia!
'Vegemite on toast' is a breakfast tradition aswell
as at any other time of day! It's a savoury spread
that you must apply very lightly!

VEGEMITE !

W

WOOP WOOP
is a term used for places
that are very far away!

*"That place is near WOOP-WOOP!
It's so far away!"*

WOOP
WOOP
500 KMS

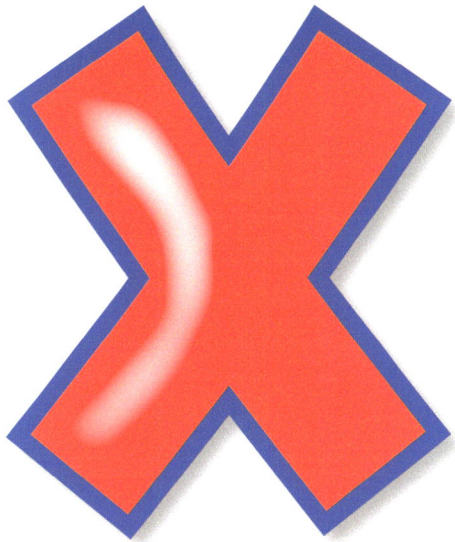

XANTIPPE

is a small rural town located in Western Australia! Infact, **XANTIPPE** is the only place in all of Australia that starts with an X!

Y

YOBBO is the term given to a loud, loutish, hooligan with bad fashion sense, usually found in a pub or at a sports game. Also known as a Bogan.

YABBIES are freshwater crayfish! Their colours vary depending on the water they live in!

YABBY is an Aboriginal word.

Z

ZZZZZZZ

Learning the alphabet from A to Z can make you feel **ZONKED!**

ZONKED is Aussie slang for tired or sleepy!

(In Australia, **Z** is pronounced **ZED!**)

THE END!

A B C D E
F G H I J K
L M N O P
Q R S T U
V W X Y Z

www.ingramcontent.com/pod-product-compliance
Lightning Source LLC
Chambersburg PA
CBHW040811300326
41914CB00065B/1490